Coherer

Verge Books, Chicago

Alicia Cohen

Coherer

Copyright © 2016 by Alicia Cohen

All rights reserved

Published by Verge Books

www.vergebooks.com

ISBN 978-0-9889885-3-8

Design and composition by Quemadura

Printed on acid-free, recycled paper

in the United States of America

for

Avalee, Howard &
Robert

Coherer

Easter Island	3
Improved	4
Transformers	5
After the ice age	7
Poetry	8
Fern and spore	9
Walk	10
Gnosis and Gertrude Stein	11
Spirit	12
Cat	13
Testament	14
Elephants	15
Fall poem	17
Sunset	19
Anatomy	20

The law is not deduced

Dissertation on cleaning; or, The housekeeper's lament	25
Earthed	28
Return of summers	29
Foment's body	30
Yeti (love poem)	31
Nomad architecture	32
Cli-fi	33

Cosmology	34
Cedar	36
The fires	37
Cleis	38
Domestic	39

Infinitesimal, weird, and nothing but music

Boys don't cry	43
This lime-tree bower my prison	45
Cosmos's	48
Chemical storm nanoparticle	49
The daffodils	50
Missing winds	52
Gutenberg and internet	55
Buffalo spring	56
On my birthday	58
Labor party	60
Molecular structure of absent breath	61
Perfumey neurotoxins	62

Predation

Parable	65
Civic life	66
Magic Kingdom	67
Feudal Society vols. 1 and 2 by Marc Bloch	68

Oregon Coast by Joyce Herbst	70
Tillamook coast forest	71
Catastrophes	73
Make it new	75
Tyger	77
Properties	80
Bacteria hosts	81
Sunstorm	82
Still life	83

The Eleusinian mysteries

Cyclops	87
The sea life	88
Cyclopean masonry	92
Return	94
Orpheus	96
Techne (the dead)	97
Judgment and friendship	98
Wonders are many; or, The hunter's song	100

Coherer

Saw you hangin' from a tree
And I made believe it was me

Oh, I'm stickin' with you
Cause I'm made out of glue

—LOU REED

endlessly generated the boy arises from his surfboard . . . greeting him the little dog eagle overhead who've led the laughing base runner in the emerald zone suddenly to deorbit popping blown onto the sand. They are from the glass tube of the coherer.

—LESLIE SCALAPINO

Easter Island

bulky aliens
eat all the earth flower

food and shade
our discipline

loves
shape

Improved

this cleaning
fluid is poison
made full from forms of care

always dipping
our rags into
disaster like
the burst stars
we are

Transformers

who
am I now   winged
lungs
become oil
liquid blood mine
traffic
benzenes and sulfur

I am dinosaur breath
and forest
wet iron leaf and bone breathing still
circulating the Gulf

the Caspian Sea's
wing of the pelican

I am black and sticky
seeking from
earth
a fast heaven

ice mountains melt into
past
new world

all at once
full of feet
wheel and wind sound
wandering

my animal has a body and breathes
now
in what we will call
the city
engines of a criminal turn turn
off tuning into fossils' briefness

After the ice age

now is room void enough
for a poem
to illumine my ear to a glass sunshadow swimming and
    shimmering
in on the white walls

framing the port-hole
open to the cedar-
time memory

gone forests cut
down and reseeded

before this world
upends   a late ice age

us weird snow wanderers with mouthfuls of air   poems
mouthfuls of air   homes
dank and sapphire fiery
lit domes

Poetry

written in a
wreath wild nut
brown inhabiting stone
case timed frigate frigid fret
music stone undo to burnish
and brandish soup dish and
weird welt upswinging tuned
and roundabout kindling
swerve in hightide to
swing swells upon
that spindle

Fern and spore

this arc'd frond
mounts respiration's
wild reprise

Walk

swings bodies and bends mind back
to starry naught
thought

Gnosis and Gertrude Stein

room cup key
hidden on the surface
unmistakable and evident

Spirit

this mark'd song
mounts respiration's
wild reprise

Cat

the world is fat
a beautiful fat
zero for nomads

Testament

a body and a question
you cannot answer   no
love but housed in mourning

Elephants

a hut on a hill
receiving storms and starlight

live here
another year
spellbound
family wrought with
the gaze gazed into

stormwatchers in the full disaster
fashioned of loves
we name with a
word stirring like a crow or sparrow
spirit
flying away with mine   nothing but a beetle

always kidnapping each other for food or pleasure
in error is desire's arrow

aster flowers in Chernobyl feed roe deer
wild boar bed in abandoned homes under bats' exit
into night diving among eagle owls and lynx in the moonlight

gated places and prisons
wild full of our relations and lovers

long trunks caressing bleached bones
we feel
losses' endlessness as
elephants grieve kin

come home
is shipwrecks shining full of love's account

Fall poem

—FOR PASCALE

I would like a light for my bike
a bike for each   leaf   for each
is a lantern
festival falling
falling on these wide tar streets

the perfume of *sweet rot* ring ring

honk honk   gold   golden and gone
from green in the hello gala now hatching
now

blooms
goodbye to summer and one
two three four and our great great grandparents
and the great peace and all wars
the grand mystery eye blooming traced by our hands
holding each other not far

from the ocean's deepestdark sands and stars dying
and born into   you
studying texts of this festival of death and candy watermelon

fairies and doctors   a witch and a princess
and a pirate with hooks   it is

a sorrow storm and an unenvisionable yes
that makes us to know the letters in bless
b - l - e - s - s *sip* they fall from wild trees that wander
toward sun and root down
to bloom   yes

may each have a bike may we all have long life for a moment
   right now

breathe in
and make green and out turning red
orange gold
even all the dead poets
breathe in   out yellowy gold

Thank you thank you
to each dear sweet leaf
and all that ever have fallen
we imagine gathered and wreathed

Sunset

—FOR HAROLD

the sun is always setting
on owls
roosts soaring
reams of data
collected
measure the death
of the sun
measure of music and day
where pollen is lit
under the cherry tree
in blossom
follow one mote with eyes
and grab at the particle as it passes
everyone
has seen it happening
all full of the clustering
and phenomenal

Anatomy

we have always lived here
in this strange snow
once
we were winged
zooplankton

and dinosaur

hulking home

keeps burning
us to ash

who is it who grows again
out of stars

difficult to attend to our fragile breath
with care

for each one wisps away

like infants
grow old and slip back into earth

I live in the river
burning

mouth full
of air and hungry crocodile teeth

The law is not deduced

[T]he historian must break with the monopoly over history granted to the cognitive regimen of phrases, and he or she must venture forth by lending his or her ear to what is not presentable under the rules of knowledge. Every reality entails this exigency insofar as it entails possible unknown senses.

—JEAN-FRANÇOIS LYOTARD (trans. Georges Van Den Abbeele), *The Differend: Phrases in Dispute*

Our flourishing industry in implements of murder is filling the vaults of New York's banks with gold. And a dollar that is not being used to make a slave of some human being is not fulfilling its purpose in the capitalistic scheme.

—HELEN KELLER, *Strike Against War*

Dissertation on cleaning; or, The housekeeper's lament

This piece of wax; it is quite fresh, having been but recently taken from the beehive; it has not yet lost the sweetness of the honey it contained; it still retains somewhat of the odor of the flowers from which it was gathered; its color, figure, size, are apparent; it is hard, cold, easily handled; and sounds when struck upon with the finger.

—RENÉ DESCARTES, *Meditation II* (trans. John Veitch)

PART I

records strewn
juice drips
mildews undo the tiling
cat poop to be scooped
red fungus's weekly rings
soft bed piled with clothes
we inhabit
cleaning
I found a pine cone on the carpet

full of dust and insect dung
bursting over the flatwool mat
it smells and is a barbarous atlas for
the swelling cedar outside under grey cloud

drawn out to its heavy air
step around a dry needlerug floor
step soft
sweet blooms
pinefumes

round trunkmass and
the rough tune of bark's
touch encounter brown skin
woody air/song
tender aquifer hush flowing up

root system waterway and bole's ten thousand thousand
   gallons
gush up   to   fly off
bud   needle and cone
molecule order's mute mutinous din

I'm tumultuous hauling my innerwaters by foot
crunching last summer's hot scales circling the cedar

PART II

housekeepers fix mess and wreck
unnoted among
galaxies of perfume earth

cabbage berry mold sweet milk baby
hunger body thought dandelion dung philosophers
full of silence ordering discourses

to clean
is to be
we
being
making messes
servants of rooting
our water sacs
dwelling diary trash piles
and every human pleasure
coupled to refuse

will's a mess
      mind suffers and
joy too
occupant of
the housekeeper's duty and
rigid industry

bodies sail
winging mist deep dirt wind blast
turning toward warm flows
assembling clocks merrily seducing rust

redgold stardust

Earthed

poetic transport delivers us
to the airy actual   bats
redo Range Rovers as ash wings
become   songs'
echolocation
soundway's corrupt sweet dipping and soaring to
birdsong city seek overstorey waterfilled

Return of summers

early summer sun is eternal
return's glistening pool
party late summer's hot death
everyone expects alone together
and the hollow feeling
of being
on the volcano

Foment's body

under open sky
open sky

it's unseeable
the unsalable bell of scent groves

I cannot
run from
being
enmeshed
    in all
these many infinities
leaving   traces
of having
been

Yeti (love poem)

your dark wood eyes are primeval boundless
your voice lilts in on elemental airs

where it is so dark at night
I don't know who you are

but glimpse you careening through the clearing
in no time

Nomad architecture

in the British Museum a pine sprouted
mid library
first the seed underground   then the soft rubber sprout

up to the oak desks lacquered in 1856
pine gases
the shone-green shining lit needles
giant roots moving imperceptible
watered by authors lining the fragile shelves

gentle slow through the dome
built to share the beauty of heaven's
drought summer and seas swelling with plastic

Cli-fi

longing is the only
belonging

all children wander thoughtlessly
into the street
sweet grassway
windstorms carry forest breath in tides over the whole earth

spider's web phones
cougarhabitat innercity

there are no weeds
everything exists
future flowers

notes of the long song
inhabitation's togetherness

Cosmology

"I prefer not to," he replied in a flute-like tone.
   —HERMAN MELVILLE, "Bartelby the Scrivener:
   A Story of Wall Street"

1.

as the handsome cars pass
destroy the world

flip into a monstrous
failure of birds
in shadows cast by our star afar
ninety-three million miles emanating to

2.

touch leaves floating above ground sprung on
bare branches last month over glad smoking motors
roaring past

as the toxins waft off breath
balloons with flowers' return of Demeter
soil and singing bees
bring back the world of body's measure into hums

3.

honey embodiment gobbling
glory bobbing up is always
busy with being for another

which sinks and resurfaces
in every unknown evident entity
open to grief coming too
fast

4.

suffering of animal people
fills my fridge like sentences to serve

I would prefer not to
in the key of B

refusal's airy old housed vowels are
weightless wrenches for free-
ing

Cedar

Oligarchs think you alone can own the palaces
and passes to symphonies all full of   without

a great tree

in moonlight hear the raccoons scratch claw and feel paw
graze food's delight
ice shower expanse night

The fires

bikes slip near silence
and spacious sounds of the river open
at the bridge's closure
the engines turn off

cyclists' feet balance and crowd the beams
falcon calls fly from the truss
arch
shimmering as hulls pass under
the sun
blinding   eyes
made of   sunbeams
looking

Cleis

I have a beautiful daughter who looks like golden flowers, my darling Cleis, for whom I would not [. . .] all Lydia or lovely [. . .]

   —SAPPHO (trans. D. A. Campbell)

perhaps I worried you would be
so wild dear to me
you'd make
that me
flee and open storms of
we in-
deed

uncovering awoke
when in accidental yoke
I set that door in oak

stepped down
into the flawless broke

unnamed
you and you

Domestic

milk
day and day and hour and passage of light
moonlit night
scholars all
busy sitting and cooking

who is it who composes compasses in
still starry chants
lists and lists that circle back and lump in
our glad hearts yet

being awakening to the full
warhorror hovering
and rough obscurity walking

even holding this
soft small hand
appeared
like magic
and the missing

Infinitesimal, weird, and nothing but music

[E]ven though strings have spatial extent, the question of their composition is without content.

—BRIAN GREENE, *The Elegant Universe*

*The scholarly string player has a theory
of his tone the old hour listens
'I don't understand a thing you're saying
but it's terribly'—sleepily—'out of tune.'
Counting sevens an ornament unto my wound.*

—LOUIS ZUKOFSKY, "Atque in Perpetuum A.W."

Boys don't cry

    counting sevens
    an ornament unto my
wound where some songs
capture you
by hand-

made extremely large
telescopes

spy sincere multiverses
alight as a needle brushes lodestone to vinyl
hear big
bang pop
and again music of

spheres arise where there
was not you
in sorrow lies hiding tears
like turning all the people into animals
into sweet fur shapes or some shared childhood

like almost infinite two minute thirty-five second happy
livid revolution
minute and electric unprison

This lime-tree bower my prison

—FOR JÉRÔME CORNETTE

lift the soul, and contemplate
With lively joy the joys we cannot share.
My gentle-hearted Charles! when the last rook
Beat its straight path along the dusky air
Homewards, I blest it! deeming its black wing
(Now a dim speck, now vanishing in light) . . .

—SAMUEL TAYLOR COLERIDGE

1.

green and aimless nobodies
we wanted more to become

help make this invisible statue of togetherness's form
our protection from cold and hurt
polish it

it is the alien home of birch leaves in wind
and invasive water oaks lit in late summer sun

which nobody turns to to be
banished to ocean speech

beckoning from beyond the rip tides
endangering floating hearts

2.

no one wants children to become poets to be
upswept in death for love of all we cannot know

and throw gold cups in the sea
faithful in the faithlessness of return

3.

we pay taxes for
each of us is stars
in families of carbon breathing wandering
through magic dusts and vacancy's infancies

it's hard here
we are often exhausted and
our loves always drown

4.

still waters
gleam

in any lost moment
a single leaf waving
moonlit
among dead stars shining back lit
in animal eyes
so boring
it opens
up the yawning
silver
mine

Cosmos's

belonging to what
silence is   songs
quaking into world
unexpected poppy
contemporary perpetual
weedlessness

Chemical storm nanoparticle

Janus face
exhaust pipes
twin recipient of everything
we make
plastic particles wandering hilltop deepsea paved grove
meet at your desk

your field
look up at the sun
being up in the sky
hidden in electrochemical
sun storm fleck
being fleck
and fret
made of short breaths
linked and sunlit

The daffodils

lonely golden fat voice
wandered saying goodbye
wolf child of Tehran
wolf milk and the boy licked

wolf tongue
cloud baby
born to loss's
fullness and host to weird worlds of really
setting out to sea

come
to share messes
wreck come
earth storm foodie
eating sunfired kale milky
way on clover among bees' disappearing
inside the psychotoxic fungicide pesticide herbicide brew
of perfection's exclusions from
sharing wolf kings and CEOs jocund
home to mycelium

shortly

fruiting bodies flash like strangers and other
   beloved

hosts of the inward eye

nation of spiders

webmakers and newborn eaters

Missing winds

1.

when Coleridge fled to the Mediterranean
he kept lengthy notes of the boat's sails in the wind

sail in still air awakens
vibrations   arise
the movements
     matter

sailor calling box falling smacked water seal bark and dive
bump the poet's ear
ear sails
taut drums move in return
make
full bubbles burst
in visions
arise   eyes
closed
to Coleridge in quoting

2.

a world
composed
where the harbor smells
silver fish and salt water sun
and the bell of every voice calls out and echoes
in noon's airy vacuum

on that harbor sea his hand
sliced out a curving
and infinitely black line on a whitish page
flowering thus unstoppable
it engulfs him here
in the lost harbor
where every ship is all frigate

3.

California shipyard expanse aircraft
carriers
waves salt
on the beach beside freeways reading
His long treks through England and Germany trod path
black earth wet step boots
silenced by the roaring trucks to come

tree roots make a place to step —the path of deafening
infinitely motored to stop the slow
foot and fin made bandit

Keswick, Cumbria
so dark at night
silence riots outside
too quiet to think Coleridge wrote
inside coming storms
the trees in squally wind

Gutenberg and internet

spiders' webs' intricate collaboration
with fly-time and star

joint
of the leg
thin hair precise
weaving
skill each spider
unearned too
honey flower bee

and amoebas'
skill steadies the nerve net's
movement to center
the computer
boxes flower out

Buffalo spring

To live's to fly
all low an' high

—TOWNES VAN ZANDT

in Buffalo the spring swells over
the cement foot and
winds gather at the river gather
buds off hand planted bushes and bulb flowers
overpower stenches of the historic dumps

here sudden crows
blueblack tempests
take from tree to tree
as copious as
sorrows of the world are

springs water molecules inhabiting aspen and oak
and willow as abundant as each black thread on each
crow feather and each cell of each thread of the wings
grow
live fly
and fly they are
everywhere and winged

being
cold

called to exterior's
demotic augury
among grey clouds
squall voices tree chorus
dark wing gale settling in a tree
caw

no stopping reading this calling
to call back I am here and hear and come
outside
there is an outside
it's our share and where
we find our silky wingedness
and friends

On my birthday

I have a portable metal box unfixed to places
inside it

I opened it and watched The Clash

today is my birthday 2013
Bankrobber glimmers and traces
London 1978

this world now is gone and was even then
see my Charons all unstill making sweet
river way
Strummer's open song
engulfs
the inverse-anger heart
to point at and
hover over
the "world" with wings
   away
and
rains in the American desert

dates fabricate mars I celebrate

I awoke to a real mean Reaganomics
sand and palms and bikes
tv and all
the cruel objects made brutal-footed in easy desire
cars and plastic to trash
the ocean laps

under the sea anchor of inverse-light
I grow toward
the birth
that is
arising in

phoning the dead world
on guitar   video   stream

Labor party

sleepy days
new baby nomad
milk share

I remember in dreams what I'd dismissed
awake and remember again dreaming

the flower in the garden
blossomed yellow with red striping
fired in air

kiln world
hot at work

Molecular structure of absent breath

the enduring   gone
is voiced
in chemical wash's hushed stinging
atmosphere

current in
a mouthful of air is
poem's persisting
nanoreef soup of ion and dendrite strike dendrite
gust of stormy molecular
import inflates

riding down the red throat passage to a
lungful bowl churning wild honeycomb air sac mosaic
elation
spring daylight icy earth
flowerbed gardeners long dead city galaxy daylight scent
   narcissus
hyacinth

Perfumey neurotoxins

cancer is tending
synthetic perfumes' "honey"
shrieking molecules
filled with ontic silence
devised to silence

everything
we eat is web's fume
vibration and calls out
to tell us we are
meant to be here
among insects and
hopping spores who emit the great
fungal odor songs

Predation

*Wonders are many, and none is more wonderful than man; . . .
the light-hearted race of birds, and the tribes of savage beasts,
and the sea-brood of the deep, he snares in the meshes of his woven
toils, he leads captive, man excellent in wit. And he masters by
his arts the beast whose lair is in the wilds, who roams the hills.*

—CHORUS, *Antigone* (trans. Richard Claverhouse Jebb)

*The One and the Other is the true origin of thought as possession-
taking of an object.*

—MARTIN HEIDEGGER, *Frühe Schriften*
(trans. Rüdiger Safranski)

Parable

native of this Titanic demesne I like to squat an unlit closet
to perceive my clan and consider corners with fanatic
concentration loading the cupboard to breaking

supremely forlorn and more and more forlornly huddled
cyclones crack open tiny wave-like doors

I am frightened of storms
the cataclysm coming
and this time my dynasty's acts come fragile and actual
not what we wanted when we set out to grasp the Real

authors and root
storm catchers of the incalculable palace
we are all called
to shelter and account
under starlight night's particular type of infinite open

Civic life

these streets
trued with airy tools
warm on the shoulder
the wind we swim in and with which air
we dead speak

let me tell you of my time—
metal roams free full of flame
retardant plastic and leather
stenching the ear

their exhaustpiped breath burns the lungs of song
and spree on their errands like speed hunting itself
if the mountain lion
were free of feeling and full of unlimitedness's
extreme extent

here the mountain lion is to be gone from the world
freeway
cars pose in mad dinosaur armature

Magic Kingdom

*"There is just one moon and one golden sun
and a smile means friendship to everyone"*

—"IT'S A SMALL WORLD" DISNEYLAND RIDE

Anaheim peppers   produce
isle
basket

driving
signs along the I-5
picture families
fleeing across the freeway

hurtling metal
rivers of poison
tailpipes
and
shadeless fields sprayed daily

feudal
magic real persisting

Feudal Society vols. 1 and 2
by Marc Bloch

implication's poem ocean
implicate order
on the island inlet of mind
open to seas of castles and
fortifications in ruin
foggy bank stretching moors of York
to prairie and Cherokee
linked in moonlight
moonlight eaten by nightshades sporing overseas
in lost worlds we carry the germ

lyric poet knights errant
music time made afar
from ravage

me I sit in a house hot with coal fire
smoking at Boardman, Oregon many long hours away from
    here

my house-heat will
be the breath of beings I never meet
after the end of our burning world

errant war by gentle folk and poets'
fangs all soft desire for sweet things and kindnesses
and wanderlust with a lance over epochs and poetries
companion song complicit
son and daughter on fire burning
with not knowing and death
and the impenetrable next breath

Oregon Coast by Joyce Herbst

document of what was
inexhaustible
oyster pickers
dwarfing forest
long canoe

vast
work of recording
vast
goodbye

never to consent
at the outset nor
in the aftermath

what happened is all we have
not done

reparations
haunting
a kind of calling

Tillamook coast forest

evidence of our unsolitary death
in piles and
fiery wisps
a hundred hundred horses and ten ten thousand
    mesohippuses
full of missing

being in
my old canoe

my seagreen daughter's eyes are destined to loss's fullness
I cannot hold to forever's ocean

   smoke proof
       the love of the world
the bird's held   gaze
winging past

long long to buoy
each pierced being flies

in fury suffered
at the cusp
approach of the wilderness
undoing the cherished forest
Tillamook attended to
with reckless laboriousness
municipal fortune

suppression stoked
storm burns beginning in '33
forest fire so fierce it disappears
blare of attention's anger is deafening
and recurs like
lumber grows a logic
that turns hot

Catastrophes

rest
in misuses's
endlessness off-
spring and words
plants   green beans
and kale and so forth

back
to the seas over all the earth
and the fish wandering
in my dreams you
died in and in my dreams
my dead friends
surface

what we know
in looking at the world
cannot
put to rest

the dead who wake us
in

spring
equinox at the bottom of the cliffs
near my childhood
home stones cover the beach
and roll with the waves singing
these tidepools are poor

for sea cucumber and sea snail and anemone
seem gone
  it's a speck of nothing
so small you can see
the world we love is full of fishes going into stars
full of spores' wreck
amino acids
and puns and rhymes
are all bad desire's good
airs' sweet smell

ocean breeze in
labworkers and truckers and us all
full of animals peering out

Make it new

―FOR ALLISON COBB

so much depends upon
inedible plastics
flooding the food chain
microshard and plankton

albatrosses burst with our
refuse
to see
trash
in each item we long for
to escape the tender cycle
wrapped in enclosures
of the cellular wilderness bizarre trespass

collecting our thoughts for an
icky potlatch
weed whacker thread   brush   razor

as weird beings
evolve to eat plastic
even this moment
rests for sorrow's
incalculable yes

Tyger

When the stars threw down their spears
And watered heaven with their tears

—WILLIAM BLAKE

tiger inside
there is a lamb inside
a turkey vulture inside
a swan

a worm inside
a newborn Burmese Hare inside an alligator inside a crane
    inside

a butterfly inside

flying—

houses fall to the ground
a gourd cracked backwards
seed erupts into pine
wreck shot through with shoots
pine fumes swim in
abandoned

girl put in a pit
tied hands
dirt in her lungs and stomach
humans put some of their children in pits

the why of this woe
is more mysterious
to us than time's interior real
and the description of space's extent
as if a pit or a cage we made
to contain being

a tiger inside
a lamb inside
a vulture inside
a swan
a worm inside
a cottontail inside a newborn crocodile inside a crane inside
a Mourning Cloak Butterfly
inside flying

cloud cover coming over and going
over and inside
world of
beast's teeth and fang primordial sea
swimming and suctioned and eating each other

eating each other and
not eating choosing not eating
and calculating
the death of the sun and
the hour of our hot-fire supper

Properties

the sea's a buoy
   like love
yawning and gaping
home

to beings
deep and
longing

eggs or live
births on the sand
near the colony

Bacteria hosts

being nothing but a wisp of
bird song in the firetime

made of sorrow
like a sparrow

their soft cheeks
heir to
their dear needs

Sunstorm

today is the first grey day all week
the sun
is inside
shining
and screaming
I am running in circles

mama unsayableness is the condition
we who love the sun so
stretching back in the morning
to the early sun gatherers
protophyta
glistening waters

Still life

AFTER WILLIAM WORDSWORTH

spore leafy chemical wilderness
jungle flower pod pollen frog elation
winds with vapor and sunshadow
mimicked in databanks cricket song
lit hermetic google storehouse of galaxy gas and dusty
loneliness of summers' last glance

pores of seasand bubbling
sites the borderland crabs dwelling
underearth history veins
of coal
and bulbs of daffodil bubble up
ranging the hillside
grave molecule and alone together blind singing
beings make their material eyes
before the seeable

The Eleusinian Mysteries

[T]o make Demeter's holy grain sound and heavy, when you first begin ploughing . . . bring down your stick on the backs of oxen as they draw on the pole-bar by the yoke straps. Let a slave follow a little behind with a mattock and make trouble for the birds by hiding the seed; for good management is the best for mortal men as bad management is the worst.

—HESIOD, *Works and Days* (trans. H. G. Evelyn-White)

The Eleusis phenomenon is not yet completely understood. However, factors of geomorphology, warm water masses in the summer and warm winds might be responsible for its summer climate. According to Kassomenos and Katsoulis (2006), based on 12 years of data (1990–2001), the industrialization of west Attica, where at least 40% of the industrial activity of the country is concentrated, could be the cause of the warm climate of the zone.

—WIKIPEDIA

We were in the lovely meadows and plucking blossoms with our hands; crocuses mingled, and iris, and hyacinth, a marvel to behold, and narcissus, that the wide earth bare, a wile for my undoing. Gladly I gathered them when the earth gaped beneath, and therefrom leaped the mighty prince, host of many guests, and he bare me against my will, despite my grief, beneath the earth, in his golden chariot.

—*Hymn to Demeter*, ANONYMOUS, possibly seventh century BCE (trans. Andrew Lang)

Cyclops

I thought I had one eye
but now I see myself
doubled on a funerary mask
leading the lost goat herd
to the mountains

we are monsters
sibling to lichen and stone
love the big
bang's first stars shining

The sea life

There rises a watchtower beheld of men afar. There sleep the mighty dead as in life they slept, warriors and princes of high renown. A pleasant land it is in sooth of murmuring waters, fishful streams where sport the gunnard, the plaice, the roach, the halibut, the gibbed haddock, the grilse, the dab, the brill, the flounder, the mixed coarse fish generally and other denizens of the aqueous kingdom too numerous to be enumerated.

—JAMES JOYCE, *Ulysses*, Chapter 12

1.

I love the way my hair flows
I wash it in the ocean water
and treat it with teatree soap
with olive and lavender

and make small braids that open
to wavelets flowing over round
shoulders
and slippery skin

or a mass of rings and looped curl that combover
in a permed bowlcut

we dye purple and fuchsia spikes in mohawk
beet juices and ochre
ginger rough longing
fires tingles and work prickles
that pinch the phenotypic skin
looping men in women skin

caress
   across
an unsaleable field
the braid is method's electric erratic
nipple and warm flush of spikes' rush
waves of repulsion
and in-
verse
desire

all this undersea
theater memory is captivating
come taste watery
loves' many charms
baby belly smell and soft drum kiss
or charged
to make something dear

the teens are part jellyfish part Cyclops
rude and knocking

trudging through the glassy store
in the underground mall lit with neon lights all these shiny
    black spiky heels
all these anemone soft lips painted purple and pink and
    green
screaming for a luscious return
an unpoisoned
sea

2.

her rattail morphed from a mullet
but she grew it again and tinted it canary
for cornrows
that float
behind as we swim in the silent black sea
eyes open in salt
water fluid form
amoeba dream and longing
jellyfish prick and sting
to be aphid eaters

all my ancestors

underground
seabed

live trees
wave upon
their carbon form foot
ghost tale oil well in this poem's foot also

all the fish gills on my neck closed up in the womb
where Sapphic fragments and the monotheist songs
weave and braid the shape of care the shape of my halo head
my nerve net
rhopalial lappets love light
and sing gravity in waves
mold fleshy hearts

Cyclopean masonry

Cyclops, if any human being asks of you how your eye was so hideously put out, say that Odysseus, despoiler of cities, did it.

   —HOMER, *The Odyssey*, Book 9 (trans. T. E. Shaw)

the sorrow of my monstrousness
overtakes me like a watchtower
I am struck
with sorrow's javelin sitting on the side of the road

nobody is here
on the path
among reeds and wren song
fishful waters move in a bed behind me
my ear
   in fennel salt air catches
the ocean waves

afar
brown mist smoky encircling
freighters and frigates
I cannot make it glisten again unambiguous blue
even in song
the polluters follow me everywhere
like a gas

encompassing our eons of plunderers' endowment
whose war songs will not
slip into the sea
lastly like Odysseus and Iphigenia
swimming among old walruses

I see his gold curls waving mama kiss me
he is not there behind me arising
to kiss   I cannot
really   see   him
or my black eyelash green sea-eyed daughter
they are so quick and divine
with nasturtium breath
whispering to
   give back what was stolen from me
majestic nothing
strong slippery real
sweetfat relations

Return

on a vessel I reached
Greece for the first time and died and then died
come round to the long Aegean sky

in a mask and snorkel I
saw azure plastic sacks swarming
the urchin badlands

an underworld arrested in great tanks
beside the Mysteries in Eleusís

Hades massive refinery
oil tankers offshore black smoke pluming visible
from the ruined center of the temple

where people sleep and dream
maybe of Demeter or Persephone's return

I awoke with my children wearing their
backpacks and we were wandering again

for healing
the sick people walked from the Acropolis
on Ἱερὰ Ὁδός road
now a river of exhaust and racket
called highway EO8

Orpheus

in motion
mirror
nothing
and
speak
the opposite self
flowers in songs'
eye
the enemy's

patience and
care
from the dirt
earth and secret
being we all die
inside
of

Techne (the dead)

I usually take the path through town
that steeps in technology's
odor flows of exhaust fume
and a brown haze on the world
but this morning I listened to the dead
speaking on streams from the web
gold-lipped Reznikoff awoke in broke earphones as I rambled
down the road cold
winter sun morn
this sidewalk (1911)
and a merry numberlessness

Judgment and friendship

the goddess's figurative eye
sits

on wild blossoming lotus sizeless
in starry forever
honey imagining

not to know and to
point
a proper infinite finger

at details and ever particular
sufferings become pleasure and its

inverse remembrance
sandcastle at the edge of the pacific
sun setting over glistening water and
sitting on the sand noting single glistenings
like Achilles with his bloody sword
weeping for his friend

home
is no stillness
in the world
the unspeakable
pollutes
the underworld undoing
hearts

tugging
slow and on bodies' over time
disappearing

Wonders are many; or, The hunter's song

Monstrous, a lot. But nothing
More monstrous than man.
For he, across the night
Of the sea, [...]
puts out
In winged and whirring houses
And the noble [. . .] unspoilable tireless earth,
He rubs out; with the striving plough
[. . .]
And the world of the gaily dreaming birds
He ensnares and hunts . . .

    —CHORUS, *Antigone* (trans. Hölderlin
    and David Constantine)

1.

the canary's song has a smell
so small in its molecule cloud and
a beetle's breath is forests' exhale

jungles emit the lung of body's turn into
our wild lair
long hair   milk and kissing

sunlight flies from sun in the silent black storm's distance
   precise

to become catastrophic
encounter on the pine needle surface
on the old oak spring green leaf
struck with morning and return

everything we can know
about hunting wit
love's procession courts it
court of anger and sorrow
to hunt the meaning of number we
name blind spot and invisible
blind spot not seen   hunger is deafening

2.

O, the sweet dexterity to be
captured and beholden by beasts
moles map kumquat bee even
bacteria full of corrective emptiness's presence
we don't know her
we don't know that wren warble
we won't know the touch of the Parsnip Web Worm
not knowing your hand

not knowing the taste of cinnamon in coffee
not knowing the meaning of the book
don't know what you'll say
or the peoples who inhabit the forest
or what happened on the ridge

and I refuse to go there in my indefinite dress
with all the children who will be born
and how they may come
    their bodies
to adorn

Acknowledgments / About the Author

With great thanks to Peter O'Leary and John Tipton. Without them this book would not be here now and would not be as it is. To Tom Fisher who put aside his own writing to make it possible for me to finish this book. These poems were first read aloud and I would like to thank my hosts, the Margin Shift Collective (Seattle, Washington), the Athens Center (Athens, Greece), The Switch (Portland, Oregon), and Spare Room (Portland, Oregon).

Alicia Cohen was born in 1970 in San Diego, California, and grew up a stone's throw from the Pacific Ocean. She attended Reed College, in Portland, Oregon, where she began reading Reed alumni poets, including Philip Whalen and Leslie Scalapino. She helped run a college poetry magazine, Small Press Collective, and wrote her senior thesis on the poetry of George Oppen.

She enrolled in the Poetics Program at State University of New York, Buffalo, in 1994, studying with Charles Bernstein, Susan Howe, Robert Creeley, Jill Robbins, Keith Sanborne, and Tony Conrad. There she established and edited a journal of in-process manuscripts, *Curricle Patterns*. She received her PhD, with a minor in Media Studies, writing a dissertation on experimental realisms and the sense of the visible in Emily Dickinson, Robert Duncan, Leslie Scalapino, and Jack Spicer.

In 2000 she returned to Portland and helped found and run the collective arts space Pacific Switchboard.

She has published two prior books of poems, *bEAR* (Handwritten Press, 2000) and *Debts and Obligations* (O Books, 2008), which was a finalist for the Oregon Book Award. In 2004 she produced *Northwest Inhabitation Log*, a multimedia installation and opera. Recently, she has lived in Athens, Greece, where some of these poems were written, and also Bergen, Norway, with Tom Fisher and their two children, Pascale and Harold.